Questions AND Answers

TRANSPORT

Philip Brooks

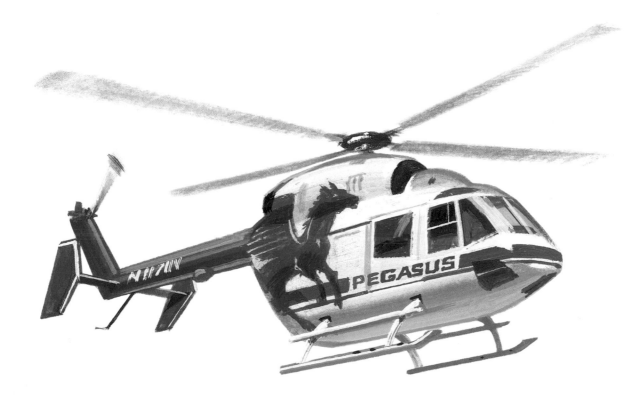

KINGFISHER
Kingfisher Publications Plc
New Penderel House
283–288 High Holborn
London WC1V 7HZ
www.kingfisherpub.com

First published by Kingfisher Publications Plc in 2001
10 9 8 7 6 5 4 3 2 1

1TR/0301/TIM/UNV/128MA

A CIP catalogue for this book is available from the British Library.

ISBN 0 7534 0546 6

Printed in China

Author: Philip Brooks
Editor: Hannah Wilson
Production: Caroline Hansell

Picture credits:
p9 br Science Photo Library; p23 b Princess Cruises

Contents

Early Transport	4
Cars	6
Racing Cars	8
Trucks	10
Special Vehicles	12
Trains	14
Bicycles	16
Motorbikes	18
Boats	20
Ships	22
Submarines	24
Hovercraft and Hydrofoils	26
Balloons and Airships	28
Aeroplanes	30
Gliders	32
Helicopters	34
Spacecraft	36
Unusual Transport	38
Index and Answers	40

Early Transport

Before the invention of the wheel about five thousand years ago, few people travelled far from home, and when they did, they went by foot. Gradually, people learned to tame and ride animals such as horses and camels, but it was the wheel that enabled people to transport large loads with ease, especially when good roads were built.

How did early people transport heavy weights?

Many structures of the ancient world, such as the pyramids in Egypt, were built with huge stones that could weigh several tonnes each. We do not know for certain how people moved these stones to the building sites. They may have dragged the stones over wooden poles laid on the ground (above) or made sledges, mounted on wooden runners. It is possible that they laid wooden paths to help the sledges move more smoothly.

What was the 'ship of the desert'?

The camel was called the 'ship of the desert' when it was used in the deserts of Asia and northern Africa to transport both people and goods. Camels were prized for their stamina – they could survive long periods with little food or water. One-humped dromedaries and two-humped Bactrian camels were both in use by 1500 BC. Camels are still used today for transport.

Ceramic rider from China around 80 BC

What is a 'travois'?

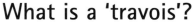

The native people of North America were often on the move, hunting and gathering food. Many used a 'travois' – a simple sledge – to transport their goods. They tied two teepee poles to the harness of a trained dog and strung their baggage between the poles.

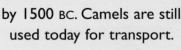

How did people manage before the invention of the wheel?

Some rich people were carried on 'litters' – platforms held up by parallel poles (left). Heavy loads were carried by pack animals – mules or donkeys in Europe and llamas in South America.

How did horse collars help transport heavy loads?

In the past, when horses dragged loads, they wore throat harnesses, which put great pressure on their windpipes, making breathing difficult. The Chinese solved this problem when they invented a padded collar that fitted around the horse's shoulders and neck, away from the windpipe. This collar enables horses to pull loads up to four times as heavy.

Can you ride without stirrups?

Yes! Early riders were very skilled at controlling horses with their legs and knees. Stirrups were probably invented in India around 200 BC, and they made horses even easier to control. Stirrups are loops for riders' feet and they are suspended from horses' saddles. Horses began to be used more in warfare because riders could perform the twists and turns needed in battle. Also, soldiers needed their hands less for controlling the horses and so could use weapons more easily.

Who invented the wheel?

The first wheels were probably made around 3500 BC in Mesopotamia – the land between the Tigris and Euphrates rivers (modern-day Iraq). They were made by nailing together planks of wood to form solid discs (above). They were strong but also very heavy and were used for carts and war chariots.

What were wheelbarrows first used for?

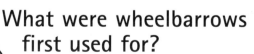

The Chinese invented the first wheelbarrows, which were simple wooden vehicles that were pushed along and used to transport people. Modern wheelbarrows are similar in design – they have one wheel at the front and two support legs at the back, but they are used to transport small loads – not people!

Quick-fire Quiz

1. Which pack animals were used in South America?
a) Horses
b) Llamas
c) Camels

2. What were early wheels made from?
a) Wood
b) Metal
c) Stone

3. How many wheels does a wheelbarrow have?
a) One
b) Two
c) Three

4. Where was the travois used?
a) Australia
b) Southeast Asia
c) North America

Cars

In just 100 years, cars have changed the world, bringing easy, convenient transport within the reach of ordinary people for the first time. There are now motor vehicles for every imaginable purpose, from ambulances and racing cars to buses and jeeps. However, all these vehicles cause problems, polluting the air and draining valuable oil reserves. Now the search is on for cars that use less energy and keep our air cleaner.

How long are limousines?

People who want to make a big impression often choose big cars – and cars do not get much bigger than a 30-metre-long stretch limousine (above). Stretch limos are usually about eight metres long and they often have problems turning street corners. Limos can often be seen ferrying the rich and famous around the world's big cities.

What was the first car?

The first true motor car was a three-wheeler built by the German engineer Carl Benz in 1885. It had a small petrol engine fitted underneath the passenger seat and this drove the back wheels to a top speed of about 15 km/h. Benz went on to build many more cars, becoming the world's first motor-car manufacturer.

Can there be a low-energy car?

Manufacturers are trying to design cars that use less energy. They have designed lightweight cars that use less petrol, as well as electric cars. However, the generation of electricity for electric cars does use coal and oil, so these vehicles are not as low-energy as they seem. One day, we may ride around in solar-powered cars that are covered with light-sensitive panels (left).

What are 'crumple zones'?

Modern cars are designed to protect passengers in a crash. The passenger compartments are surrounded by metal bars to shield those inside. But the front and rear of cars are designed to crumple in a crash, absorbing some of the impact shock. These parts of cars are called 'crumple zones'.

How fast can cars go?

By fitting jet engines to specially designed, streamlined cars, Englishman Richard Noble has built faster cars than anyone else. His most recent car, *Thrust SSC* (right), set a new record in 1997, powering to an amazing 1220.86 km/h – faster than the speed of sound.

Thrust SSC

How does the engine drive the wheels?

In most cars, the engine is at the front, but drives only the rear wheels. A long rod called a propeller shaft connects the engine to the axle of the rear wheels. Between the engine and the propeller shaft is a gearbox, which allows the driver to select a low, powerful gear for accelerating, or a higher gear for fast speeds.

What prevents cars from skidding?

In wet conditions, cars are more likely to skid. This is why car tyres have a pattern of grooves called a 'tread'. Water from the road gathers in the tread and is pushed back on to the road, away from the path of the tyre. Modern tyres are quite wide to reduce further the risk of skidding.

Quick-fire Quiz

1. How many wheels did the first car have?
a) Two
b) Three
c) Four

2. What type of engine powered *Thrust SSC*?
a) Petrol engine
b) Diesel engine
c) Jet engine

3. What sort of tyres grip the road better?
a) Wide tyres
b) Narrow tyres
c) Thicker rubber tyres

4. What provides low-energy power?
a) Hydrogen
b) Oil
c) Solar energy

Racing Cars

At the beginning of the 20th century, cars began to be designed for speed and special tracks were built for racing. Today, motor racing is huge – Formula One and Indianapolis 500 racing are multi-million dollar sports with amazing, hi-tech cars, skilled drivers, and huge support teams.

What is pole position?

Pole position is the first place on the grid from which a race starts. The position of the cars on the grid is determined during the previous qualifying circuits, when the cars are timed as they drive the course. The driver with the fastest lap wins pole position, and the others line up behind him in the order of their qualifying times.

How do racing cars 'stick' to the track?

Formula One cars are lower and more streamlined than any other type of vehicle. The shape of the body is important in two ways. First, the streamlining enables air to flow easily over the vehicle, cutting down 'drag' (air resistance) and allowing the car to go faster. Second, the air flow, aided by specially shaped wings on the front and rear, pushes the car down on to the track, holding it close to the road.

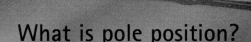

Air flow

How do racing drivers choose their tyres?

If the weather is dry, racing drivers will choose tyres called 'slicks'. Slicks are wide tyres with no tread. They grip well on dry tracks and get sticky as they warm up, helping the cars to grip roads. In wet weather, slicks do not grip well and drivers usually switch to tyres with treads.

How powerful are car engines?

Most family cars have small four-cylinder engines, designed to travel comfortably at or near the maximum road speed limit, which is 113 km/h (70 mph) in the UK. Racing cars are designed for much higher speeds. Formula One cars can reach speeds of 322 km/h and have very powerful, 12-cylinder engines.

Why can you remove steering wheels?

To keep a racing car light, streamlined and efficient, nothing is bigger than is necessary. The cockpit, where the driver sits, is very cramped, and the driver's legs nestle under the steering wheel in the front, or 'nose', of the car. To squeeze legs into the narrow nose, the driver must first remove the steering wheel.

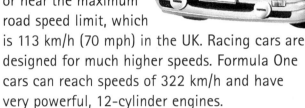

What happens in the 'pits'?

Formula One cars enter the 'pits' – service areas by the side of the tracks – at least once during races to refuel. Using special equipment, the highly skilled pit mechanics fill petrol tanks and change tyres in a matter of seconds. Also, the mechanics can usually sort out any mechanical problems very quickly.

How can we make cars even faster?

Fitting bigger engines makes cars faster, but also heavier, which slows them down. Because of this, racing-car designers concentrate on making the vehicles more streamlined, and they aim to use new materials that are very strong, but also very light in weight, such as carbon fibre. Designers use computers to try out new ideas in theory before testing them in practice on working cars.

Trucks

Early trucks were small, but as engines got larger, designers made larger trucks that could transport almost anything. Long-distance trucks have big engines, but there is still room in the 'cabs' for the drivers – sometimes there are even beds!

How many cars can you drive at once?

You can only really drive one car at once – but a modern car transporter can carry as many as nine. The upper deck of the transporter lowers at the rear so that cars can drive on to it. Then the deck is raised so that more cars can be driven on to the lower deck. Wedges and straps stop the cars moving while the transporter is in motion.

Why do so many lorries carry containers?

Containers are large metal boxes that come in two standard sizes. Lorries can be standardized to carry both sizes, and cranes are also standardized to load the containers on to ships (below).

How does a 'tipper' tip?

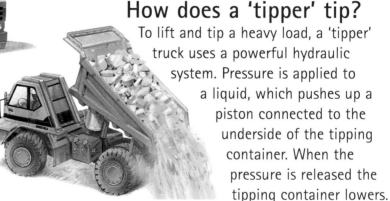

To lift and tip a heavy load, a 'tipper' truck uses a powerful hydraulic system. Pressure is applied to a liquid, which pushes up a piston connected to the underside of the tipping container. When the pressure is released the tipping container lowers.

What is a 'juggernaut'?

A 'juggernaut' is any large cargo-carrying truck. The word comes from the name of a Hindu god, whose statue was carried on large wagons in religious processions in India. It is thought that worshippers threw themselves under the wheels of these wagons. Because of this, people began to call any large truck that could crush with its wheels a 'juggernaut'.

How do you drive a 'road train'?

A 'road train' looks like a normal truck from the front, and it is only when the long train of trailers winds into view that it is clear where this impressive vehicle gets its name. It is driven like a normal truck, but when the driver needs to turn corners, he or she has to swing out in the opposite direction to the bend so that the trailers follow in the right line. Road trains are often seen in countries that have long stretches of straight roads, such as Australia.

What can trucks carry?

Trucks can be adapted to carry virtually any type of load. Tankers carry liquids, special transporters carry animals and rubbish trucks have garbage-crushing machinery. Low-loaders (above) have long, low platforms to transport other vehicles or awkward cargoes, such as logs.

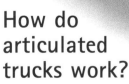

How many tonnes can a truck carry?

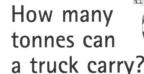

The trucks used on building sites are some of the world's biggest vehicles. Many trucks can carry more than 100 tonnes, but the latest 'monster' truck will take up to 330 tonnes – the weight of a jumbo jet!

How do articulated trucks work?

An articulated truck has two sections. The front section is the tractor, which contains the engine and the driver, and the rear section is the trailer, which carries the load. A joint links the two sections, allowing the truck to turn with more flexibility than a one-section vehicle of the same length. Cables connect the trailer's brakes and lights to the tractor, giving the driver full control.

Special Vehicles

Motor vehicles are the most adaptable form of transport. They can be used to rescue people in an emergency, harvest crops on the farm or build towering structures. Manufacturers start with the same basic machinery found on cars – wheels, gears, brakes and engines – and add any specialized equipment needed to create the best machine for the job.

What vehicles do police use?

Police forces use motorbikes to pass through busy traffic quickly, and heavily armoured vans to control riots. Police cars are fitted with flashing lights and sirens as warning signals, and they carry all kinds of equipment in their boots. Police drivers are specially trained to drive safely at high speeds.

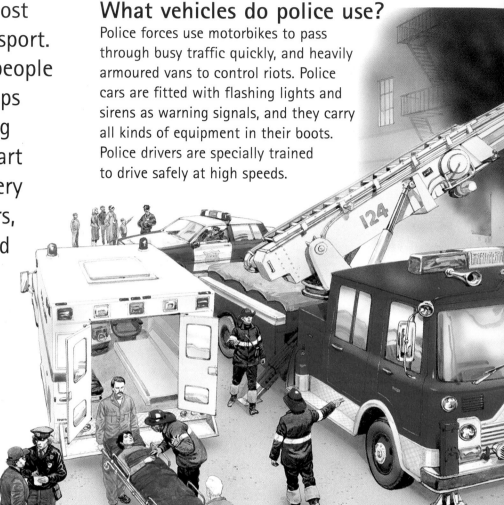

Why do tractors have such big wheels?

The rear wheels of a tractor are big in order to spread out the vehicle's heavy weight so that it does not sink into soft or muddy ground. The large wheels have thick tyres with chunky treads to provide plenty of grip on the ground. Many tractors provide power for other farm machinery directly from a connection on the rear of the tractors.

What are the special features of ambulances?

Ambulances are ordinary vans or cars fitted out with medical equipment to give emergency treatment to sick or injured people as they are driven to hospital. Ambulances must be seen and heard easily – they have sirens and flashing lights, and the word 'ambulance' is often written in reverse on the front so that other drivers can read it properly in their rear-view mirrors.

How do machines tunnel underground?

Special tunnel-boring machines dig tunnels, removing rubble with conveyor belts. If the rock is very hard, machines drill small holes and fill them with explosives to blast away the rock. Tunnels are usually lined with both steel and concrete in order to reinforce them.

How does a fire engine save lives?

There are several types of fire engine. Some have platforms or ladders that extend to just over 30 metres so that fire officers can rescue people trapped in burning buildings. Some fire engines are fitted with pumps powerful enough to deliver up to 2,840 litres of water in one minute.

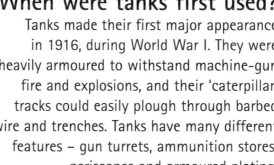

When were tanks first used?

Tanks made their first major appearance in 1916, during World War I. They were heavily armoured to withstand machine-gun fire and explosions, and their 'caterpillar' tracks could easily plough through barbed wire and trenches. Tanks have many different features – gun turrets, ammunition stores, periscopes and armoured plating.

How does a trolley bus work?

A trolley bus looks like an ordinary bus but, instead of using a diesel engine, it runs on electricity. At the top of the bus are two 'arms' with 'trolley wheels' at the end. These wheels connect to two overhead wires that supply the power. A trolley bus can only travel along the routes laid out by the power wires.

Which digger is the best ?

The JCB is the most versatile machine for digging. It has both a big scoop for picking up material from the surface and a shovel for digging holes, grabbing and other uses. The JCB has sturdy wheels as well as a series of strong steel props to prevent it toppling over when performing complicated manoeuvres involving heavy loads. Both the shovel and props are powered by hydraulics, which means that the driver can move them easily in any direction just by flicking a series of levers in the cab.

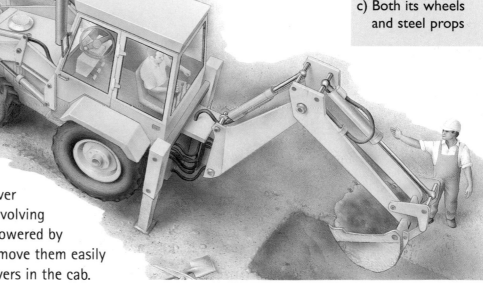

Trains

The first railway networks appeared during the 19th century in England, and soon railways were being built all over the world. They changed people's lives, allowing them to travel further and faster than ever before. The railways made it possible to transport heavy goods in bulk over land for the first time.

Were there trains before steam power?

Yes – as early as 1550, mine owners in Germany were hauling stone, coal and iron ore out of mines using trucks on tracks. The trucks were pulled by horses (above) or pushed along by the miners themselves. Most of these early railways were very short.

What were 'Big Boys'?

'Big Boys' were the largest steam locomotive trains ever built. They ran on the United States Union Pacific Railroad in the 1940s, and hauled heavy goods up the Rocky Mountains. The engines were 40 metres long, and could reach speeds of up to 130 km/h.

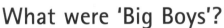

How can trains run on electricity?

Many trains are attached to overhead electric cables that supply electricity to motors that turn the wheels. The trains are linked to the cables by special connectors that use adjustable springs that take up any slack when the trains are travelling uphill.

How fast are bullet trains?

The Japanese bullet train is built for speed, and the most recent model, the JR500 (left), can reach 300 km/h. It runs on special tracks without sharp bends, which would slow the train. The French TGV (Train à Grande Vitesse) can travel at a similar speed.

How do trains hover in the air?

'Maglev' (magnetic levitation) trains are held just above the track by magnetic force. This means that when they move, the trains do not touch the track, so there is no friction to slow them. Scientists believe that one day it will be possible to travel at speeds of up to 700 km/h in maglev trains.

What was special about the *Rocket*?

The *Rocket* was a famous railway locomotive designed by British engineer George Stephenson. It was built in 1829, when a competition was held to find the best engine for the new Liverpool to Manchester railway. The *Rocket* was the winner, reaching a top speed of 47 km/h.

What were the 'Flying Hamburgers'?

In 1933, new diesel express trains (left) were built to run between Berlin and Hamburg in Germany. They were sleek, streamlined and very fast for the time, reaching a speed of 175 km/h. They became known as the 'Flying Hamburgers'. The trains were so successful that they were used on other German lines until the 1960s.

What are 'cowcatchers'?

The first American railroads were not protected by fences and cattle often wandered on to the lines. Special guards called 'cowcatchers' were fixed to the front of steam locomotives (right) to nudge the cows to safety away from the wheels. The first locomotive to have a cowcatcher was the *John Bull*, which was built in 1831.

Quick-fire Quiz

1. How fast could the *Rocket* travel?
a) 100 km/h
b) 56 km/h
c) 47 km/h

2. What don't maglev trains experience?
a) Delay
b) Friction
c) Engine

3. Where were the earliest trains used?
a) In mines
b) In cities
c) On the coast

4. Why can a bullet train travel so fast?
a) Its tracks have no sharp curves
b) It does not stop at stations
c) It carries few passengers

Bicycles

Cycling is a cheap, healthy and fun way to travel. The modern bicycle, with its diamond-shaped frame and equal-sized wheels, appeared just over 100 years ago. Since then, manufacturers have made bikes for every sort of activity – from lightweight cycles for racing to BMX bikes for tricks. There are even folding bicycles that fit into car boots!

How did bicycles begin?

A machine called the 'hobby horse' (right) appeared in the early 19th century. It had a saddle, two wheels and handlebars, just like a modern bike, but no pedals – you had to stride along the ground while the saddle took most of your weight. Hobby horses were uncomfortable and hard to ride, so they did not catch on.

Were penny farthings safe?

With its giant front wheel and tiny rear wheel, the 1870 penny farthing was not easy to ride. Many people needed steps to climb on to it, and once in the saddle, it was very easy to fall off. Even so, many people bought penny farthings. They liked the idea that, unlike a horse, the bicycle did not need feeding or looking after!

Why are racing bikes so light?

The lighter its frame, the less effort it takes to pedal a racing bike, so the faster you go. Because of this, designers make the frames with very light metals such as aluminium alloys. Narrow, treadless tyres reduce friction between the wheels and the road and also make bikes faster.

How do you ride a unicycle?

A unicycle has a saddle and two pedals, but only one wheel. Unicyclists let the saddle take their weight and then rock the pedals back and forth to balance. Beginners usually ask two friends to support them as they pedal, but after a couple of hours, riders can usually balance on their own. Skilled riders can learn to play basketball, hockey and tag on unicycles.

What makes mountain bikes special?

Mountain bikes need to be extra strong for cross-country riding. They have tough metal frames, tyres with deep treads to provide lots of grip and plenty of gears to make cycling up and down hills easy.

Quick-fire Quiz

1. What was unusual about the hobby horse?
a) It had no saddle
b) It had no pedals
c) It had no handlebars

2. How did people get on to a penny farthing?
a) By jumping
b) With steps
c) With a mechanical lifting device

3. How many people could ride the *Décuplette*?
a) Two
b) Five
c) Ten

4. Which tyres do racing bikes have?
a) Narrow, treadless tyres
b) Thick, rugged tyres
c) Solid tyres

Which bikes are the fastest?

Professional racing bikes (left), which are the fastest bicycles, need to be very streamlined. The frame, wheels and handlebars are all designed to reduce drag (air resistance). Hi-tech materials that are strong and light, such as carbon fibre, are used. Even the cyclist is streamlined – he or she wears a special helmet to reduce drag.

What can bicycles transport?

In many parts of Asia, few people can afford a car, and tricycles are popular alternatives. These vehicles often have platforms for carrying goods (right) and many riders earn money by making deliveries. Trishaws – tricycles with small seats at the rear – also provide income for riders who ferry passengers around.

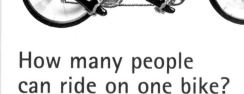

How many people can ride on one bike?

Some people like riding tandems – bicycles made for two (above), but at the end of the 19th century, some bikes were built for even more people. A number of four-seaters appeared, and there was even one French bicycle, the *Décuplette*, that carried ten people!

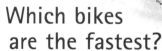

Motorbikes

The very first motorcyle, or 'motorbike', was built in 1868 and was powered by a small steam engine! But ever since Daimler made his first machine in 1885 (below), motorbikes have had petrol engines. There are all sorts of different machines from slow, economic scooters to powerful, expensive bikes that give exhilarating rides on open roads.

What's special about scrambling bikes?

Scrambling bikes are designed to be raced over muddy, bumpy courses at high speed. They have sturdy frames, thick tyres with deep treads and big mudguards to protect the rider from the mud and stones that the wheels throw up. Good suspension does help to absorb some of the shock, but scramblers must still expect a rough ride!

Why was Daimler's first motorbike made of wood?

When German engineer Gottlieb Daimler made his first petrol engine, he tested it by fitting it to a home-made wooden bicycle, creating the first-ever motorbike with a petrol engine (above). He probably used wood because many vehicles were wooden in those days, but he may have regretted his choice when the bike was destroyed by fire in 1903!

How do you 'corner' at speed?

Motorcyclists turn bends, or 'corner', by leaning into the curve. On fast bends, racing riders lean so far that it looks as if they will topple over! Professional riders know just how far to lean to give them the best route around the curve at the fastest possible speed.

How are motorbikes built for speed?

Motorbikes, especially those designed for racing, have large, powerful engines and streamlined frames to reduce drag. The seats are set back and the handlebars are low so that the rider's head and shoulders are kept down. This helps cut drag even more, enabling the rider to gain valuable seconds.

When is a bike not a bike?

When it's a trike! Three-wheeled bikes, or 'trikes', are more stable than ordinary bikes because of the support from the extra wheel. This means that trikes can be used off-road over bumpy ground. Trikes are also used for racing. Some trike owners fit large seats for extra comfort.

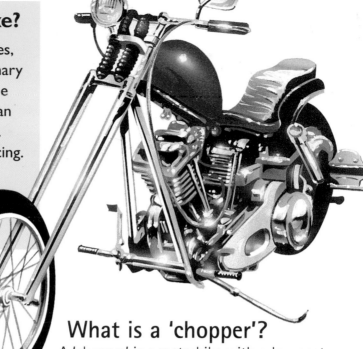

What is a 'chopper'?

A 'chopper' is a motorbike with a low seat, raised handlebars and a long fork that supports the front wheel. Most choppers do not start out like this – they are ordinary bikes that have been altered or 'customized' by their owners. The biker has to 'chop up' the original bike, alter it and then put it back together. In this way, a unique 'chopper' is made.

Which motorbikes are best in the city?

For many people, scooters or mopeds are ideal in the city. Scooters first appeared in the 1940s in Italy, but are still very popular today. They are not too expensive and are quite easy to ride. Scooters' engines are small but suitable for busy city streets where you cannot go too fast. Often the engines are covered to keep noise to a minimum.

Why were sidecars invented?

Sidecars were originally made to enable motorcyclists to carry extra passengers in comfort. But it was not long before another separate class of motor sport developed – racing motorcycles with special flattened sidecars attached! During races, the sidecar passengers must move about, shifting their weight into the best positions to keep the machines stable at speed.

Quick-fire Quiz

1. Which engine did Daimler's first motorbike have?
a) A steam engine
b) A petrol engine
c) An electric engine

2. What should sidecar passengers do in a race?
a) Shift their weight
b) Map read
c) Nothing

3. When did scooters first appear?
a) In the 1930s
b) In the 1940s
c) In the 1950s

4. Which best describes a scooter?
a) Fast and noisy
b) Small and inexpensive
c) Large and expensive

Boats

From the simplest canoe to the most powerful modern speedboat, there are now boats for every need and watercraft to suit conditions in every part of the world. In the past, people used small boats simply for getting around or for jobs such as fishing, sailing them up and down rivers and along coasts. Many of today's boats are built for pleasure – either for racing or for cruising.

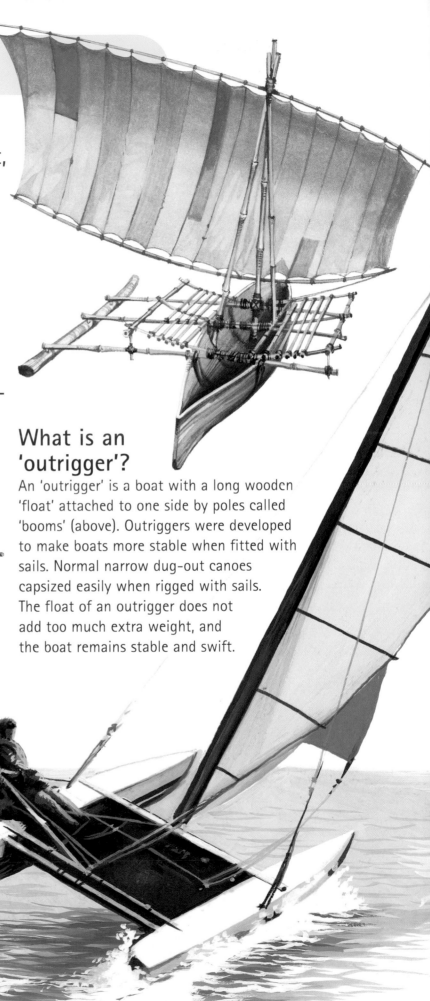

What is an 'outrigger'?

An 'outrigger' is a boat with a long wooden 'float' attached to one side by poles called 'booms' (above). Outriggers were developed to make boats more stable when fitted with sails. Normal narrow dug-out canoes capsized easily when rigged with sails. The float of an outrigger does not add too much extra weight, and the boat remains stable and swift.

What were early boats like?

The first boats were made from simple materials that were easy to find and work with. Reeds were bound tightly together to form strong, watertight boats (above). 'Dug-out' canoes were another early type of watercraft, built by prehistoric people thousands of years ago and still used today in some parts of the world. They were made from tree trunks, which were hollowed out in the middle either with stone tools or by small fires that burned away the excess wood.

Are two hulls better than one?

The hull is the main body of a boat or ship. Boats with twin hulls are called 'catamarans' (left). They are very wide and can accommodate large sails, which means that the craft can sail fast. Catamarans were developed thousands of years ago in islands of the Pacific Ocean. They are now popular for both racing and leisure.

Which boat can you carry on your back?

The coracle is a tiny, lightweight boat that has been around for thousands of years and is still used today in some parts of England and Wales. It is made from leather, which is stretched over the wooden framework, and is just big enough to carry one fisherman. When the fisherman returns to shore, he lifts out the boat, hoists it on to his shoulders and walks home.

Which boats are best for racing?

People race all sorts of boats, from tiny dinghies (small boats without decks) to large yachts. Races are organized in different classes so that boats of the same type race against each other. Most racing craft have sleek hulls made of strong, lightweight materials. Large sails are vital for speed.

Which are the fastest boats?

The fastest watercraft are speedboats, which combine powerful engines with sleek, pointed hulls. Swiftest of all is the hydroplane (above), which rises up out of the water as it speeds along. The world record for speed over water is 511.11 km/h. This was achieved by Ken Warby of Australia in a hydroplane.

Can boats sail uphill?

Yes, with help from 'locks' – sections of a canal or river that can be closed off by gates. Lock-keepers open the lower gates, allowing the boat in, and the lock fills with water until it is the same level as the water upstream. Then the upper gates open and the boat sails out. To sail downstream, the process works in reverse.

Boat sails through lower gates of lock

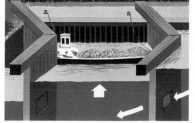
Gates close and water enters lock

Upper gates open

Ships

Ships have been used for thousands of years because it was often easier for people to sail along a river or coast than to build a road. Over time, bigger and better boats were built – from the small wooden sailing craft of early times to the vast liners and tankers of today that can sail right around the world. Since the 19th century, ships have also had engines and no longer had to depend on a good wind to get them moving.

What were the first sailing boats like?

The world's first sailing ships probably sailed about 5,000 years ago in the Mediterranean Sea and along the River Nile in Egypt. They were built by the ancient Egyptians, and had solitary square sails on tall, wooden masts (above). Their hulls were made of wood, and they were steered by a large wooden oar at the stern.

How did clippers race across the oceans?

Clippers were the fastest sailing ships of the 19th century. They often carried tea from China to Europe. Clippers had sleek, streamlined hulls, and many large sails, which enabled them to skim through the water at speed. One clipper sailed from Melbourne, Australia, to London, England, in just 85 days.

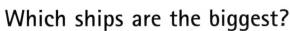

Which ships are the biggest?

The world's biggest ships are supertankers. These enormous vessels weigh up to 500,000 tonnes and are about 450 metres long. It would be possible to build tankers even bigger – up to one million tonnes – but no port in the world would be large enough to handle such vast ships.

Why did early steam ships have sails?

There were several reasons for keeping a set of sails on a steamer. By using sail power when the wind was favourable, ship-owners could travel further on a single load of coal. This meant that they saved money on coal. Also, by using sails occasionally, less coal needed to be carried, allowing more room for cargo.

Why are oil slicks dangerous?

When a tanker spills oil, the oil floats on the surface of the sea in a thin layer called a slick. The slick from a large tanker can spread out for many kilometres, and it causes damage wherever it goes. Oil sticks to the feathers of sea birds, often killing them. Oil-polluted beaches can take months to clear.

Which ship is the most luxurious?

Perhaps the most luxurious ship is the cruise liner *Grand Princess* (right). Her 12 decks offer her 2,600 passengers everything they could expect in the best hotel, and more – a casino, a theatre, a virtual-reality centre and many different restaurants. The swimming pool even has a movable roof to protect it in bad weather.

Grand Princess

Submarines

Submarines add a new dimension to warfare, enabling forces to creep up on enemy ships and launch surprise attacks. As a result, these powerful craft played an important role in both World Wars. But underwater vessels also have peaceful uses – they can be used to explore the deep, dark trenches of the oceans, discovering new species of marine life.

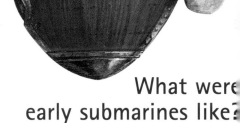

Turtle

What were early submarines like?

Early submarines were small wooden vessels that could hold only one person. They were operated by handles and foot pedals that moved two propellers – one to dive and ascend, and one to travel forwards. The *Turtle* (above), a famous early submarine, was built in 1776 during the American War of Independence to plant explosives beneath British ships.

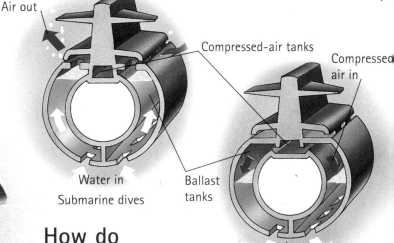

Air out
Compressed-air tanks
Compressed air in
Water in
Submarine dives
Ballast tanks
Water out
Submarine rises

How do submarines dive?

The hull of a submarine has two walls and in between these walls are large containers called ballast tanks. When the tanks contain air, the submarine floats on the surface like a normal ship. When the captain wants to dive, the tanks are gradually filled with water. This makes the vessel heavier so that it dives towards the bottom of the ocean. When it is time to surface, compressed air is released into the ballast tanks to force the water out.

Why do submarines have 'wings'?

Submarines have small 'wings' called hydroplanes. These can be moved up and down in order to help submarines climb and dive. The hydroplanes can also tilt submarines sideways to change direction.

How useful are nuclear submarines?

The submarine below is powered by an onboard nuclear reactor. The advantage of this form of power is that the craft can sail an almost unlimited distance without the need to refuel. This is useful in wartime, when vessels may have to travel thousands of kilometres from port. The drawback is that nuclear submarines are difficult and costly to service, and produce hazardous waste that needs to be treated with great caution.

Do submarines have weapons?

Most submarines are military machines used for patrolling the oceans. Submarines may have to fire at enemy craft and for this reason they are equipped with special missiles called torpedoes. Torpedoes propel themselves through the water, often over very great distances.

Torpedo

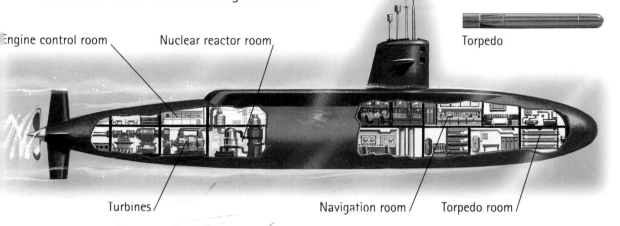

Engine control room Nuclear reactor room

Turbines Navigation room Torpedo room

Why are submarine hulls so strong?

The deeper underwater a submarine dives, the greater the pressure applied to it from the water. In 1960, when two scientists dived 10,911 metres into the Marianas Trench, the deepest underwater gorge known on Earth, their vessel, the *Trieste* (right), had to be heavily reinforced in order not to be crushed.

Trieste

How can you see above the surface?

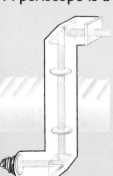

Submarines use a device called a 'periscope' to enable those on board to see what is happening on the surface. A periscope is a long tube with an angled mirror at either end. The submariner looks at the lower mirror and sees the reflected image of what is above. When the vessel dives deep, the periscope tube is lowered into the body of the submarine.

What is a 'submersible'?

A 'submersible' is a small submarine used for all sorts of underwater jobs – exploration, marine biology, repairs to oil rigs and laying pipelines. Some submersibles are remote-controlled. *Deepstar IV* (left) can operate at depths of more than 1,200 metres.

Deepstar IV

Quick-fire Quiz

1. What are the 'wings' of a submarine called?
a) Hydroplanes
b) Hydrofoils
c) Hydroponics

2. What happens to a submarine when it dives?
a) Water empties out of the ballast tanks
b) Oil flows through the ballast tanks
c) Water flows into the ballast tanks

3. What weapons do submarines sometimes use?
a) Torpedoes
b) Heat seekers
c) Submersibles

4. What is the deepest known place on Earth
a) The Dead Sea
b) The Marianas Trench
c) The South Pacific

Hovercraft and Hydrofoils

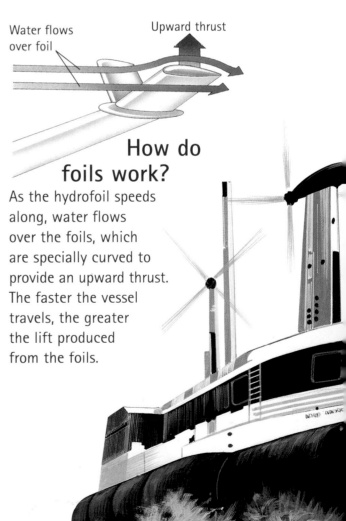

There are several types of craft that work by skimming over the surface of the sea. The most common are hovercraft and hydrofoils, which use two very different designs to keep their hulls out of the water. Hovercraft and hydrofoils are some of the fastest and most efficient craft afloat, but they do tend to be uncomfortable, and even unstable. Because of this, they are not used as much now as they were in the past.

Is this ship taking off?

No, it's a hydrofoil! It has a set of foils that lift the hull out of the water as it moves. The less contact the hydrofoil has with the water, the less drag it experiences, and the faster it can go. The vessel is efficient and this reduces the amount of fuel it uses.

Water flows over foil   Upward thrust

How do foils work?

As the hydrofoil speeds along, water flows over the foils, which are specially curved to provide an upward thrust. The faster the vessel travels, the greater the lift produced from the foils.

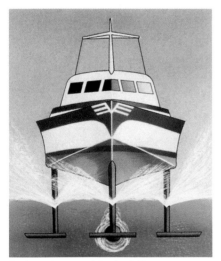

Fully submerged hydrofoil

Surface-piercing hydrofoil

Which type of 'foil' is best?

'Foils' are the underwater fins or wings beneath hydrofoils. There are two main types – those that stay submerged and those that pierce the surface of the water. Submerged foils are popular as they allow high speeds and operate well in rough seas when used with an automatic control system. Surface-piercing foils are useful when boats tip to one side as more of the foil on that side is pulled underwater and this creates forces that pull the boat upright again.

How does a hovercraft hover?

A huge fan pumps air into the area under a hovercraft (below). This creates a cushion of air on which the craft rides, or 'hovers'. Because air escapes from around the edge of the vehicle, the fan has to keep working whenever the craft is in motion to prevent it sinking into the sea.

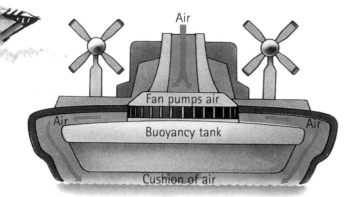

Air

Fan pumps air

Air

Buoyancy tank

Air

Cushion of air

Can hovercraft travel over both land and sea?

Hovercraft are 'amphibious' – in other words, they can ride over both land and sea. Because they have no wheels, they can even travel over bumpy terrain and marshland where it is difficult for wheeled vehicles to go. Surfaces such as ice, mud and even quicksand pose no problems for hovercraft.

What are hovercraft used for?

Hovercraft are normally used for ferrying cars and passengers. They are ideal for this type of job because they can cover short journeys at high speeds. Sometimes armed forces use hovercraft to travel over all sorts of different terrains.

Who invented the hovercraft?

Hovercraft, or 'Air-Cushion Vehicles' (ACVs), were invented by the British engineer Christopher Cockerell in the 1950s. Cockerell tested his designs with a hairdryer and two tin cans.

GH-2005

What is a hovercraft's 'skirt'?

Most hovercraft have a length of flexible rubber that goes all the way around the underside of the vehicles. This is called the 'skirt'. The skirt raises the hovercraft higher and is very flexible. This helps the craft to ride easily and smoothly over the waves. The skirt also helps to keep in the cushion of air underneath the hovercraft.

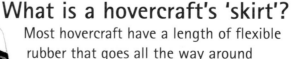

Quick-fire Quiz

1. What do the foils on hydrofoils do?
a) Protect the hull
b) Help you climb on board
c) Lift the hull out of the water

2. What do hovercraft ride on?
a) A pair of wheels
b) A cushion of air
c) A layer of rubber

3. Which word describes hovercraft?
a) Amphibious
b) Ambidextrous
c) Ambiguous

4. Why are hovercraft good ferries?
a) They are fast
b) They are comfortable
c) They are quiet

Balloons and Airships

For thousands of years, people dreamed of flying like the birds. They made flapping wings, but these never worked. Then, the Montgolfier brothers realized that the best way to fly was to make a craft that was light enough to float up into the air. The age of ballooning had begun.

Why do hot-air balloons fly?

Modern balloons have gas burners that heat the air inside the balloons. Hot air is lighter than cold air and so balloons will rise when filled with hot air. Every so often, the balloonist turns on a blast jet (right), which is next to the burner, to keep the air inside the balloon up to the right temperature.

Who was the first person to fly?

The first person to fly was François Pilâtre de Rozier. In 1783, he ascended in one of the balloons made by the French brothers Joseph and Jacques Montgolfier. The balloons were made of silk and lined with paper, and were filled with hot air. The Montgolfiers sent up a sheep, a duck and a rooster before sending up François.

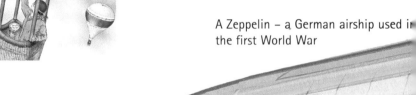

A Zeppelin – a German airship used in the first World War

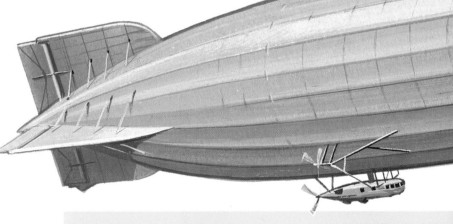

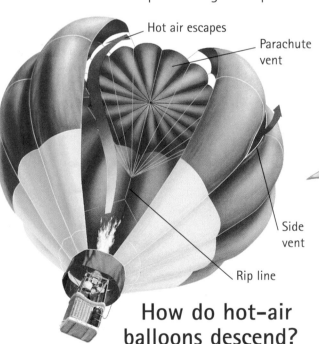

Hot air escapes

Parachute vent

Side vent

Rip line

How do hot-air balloons descend?

The balloon's bag that contains the hot-air is called the 'envelope'. At the top of the envelope is a 'parachute vent', which can be opened by pulling on a rip line that runs down into the basket. When the vent is opened, hot air escapes and is replaced by heavier cold air, and the balloon will descend. Another way to descend gradually is to stop using the burner for long periods.

How can balloons help scientists?

The first scientists to use balloons were meteorologists, who study the weather. They used balloons with special instruments to record the winds, and measure conditions in the upper atmosphere. Today, physicists send large balloons even higher into the atmosphere to measure the radiation that comes from space.

What is an airship?

An airship is similar to a hot-air balloon because it relies on being very light to get lift. But airships are not filled with hot air – instead the envelopes of modern airships contain helium, a gas that is less dense and, therefore, lighter than air. Airships have steering mechanisms and engines, which allow them to travel along scheduled routes. Balloons, on the other hand, drift along according to the air currents.

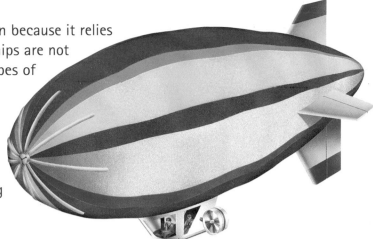

Quick-fire Quiz

1. What heats the air inside a hot-air balloon?
a) An electric heater
b) A gas burner
c) The envelope

2. How can balloons help with scientific research?
a) By predicting earthquakes
b) By measuring radiation coming from space
c) By preventing disease

3. Which part of an airship carries the passengers?
a) The gondola
b) The fuselage
c) The envelope

4. Which gas is used in airships today?
a) Hydrogen
b) Air
c) Helium

Why are airships so huge?

Airships consist of two main parts – large, balloon-like envelopes and the gondolas that hang beneath them and carry passengers. Airships are so huge because their envelopes need to be very large to hold enough gas to provide the lift needed to carry the heavy gondolas.

Why did the first airships catch fire?

The first airships were filled with hydrogen gas, which is light, but highly flammable. Unfortunately, some of these early airships were destroyed by fire. The most famous of these disasters occurred in 1937, when the *Hindenburg* (right), a 245-metre-long passenger airship, burst into flames while landing. The tragedy killed 36 people.

Aeroplanes

American brothers Wilbur and Orville Wright built the first aeroplane (below) in 1903, and flew it for only 12 seconds. Today, there are jet airliners that can fly for hours, carrying hundreds of people vast distances in comfort. It is now possible to fly faster than the speed of sound.

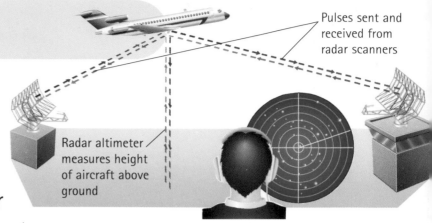

Pulses sent and received from radar scanners

Radar altimeter measures height of aircraft above ground

How are planes found in thick cloud?

Air-traffic controllers need to keep track of hundreds of aircraft in the sky in order to prevent collisions. They are not able to see most aircraft with the naked eye because of darkness, poor weather conditions and long distances. This is why air-traffic controllers use radar, which bounces radio waves off objects to work out their position. The aeroplanes appear as dots on the radar screens in the airport control tower.

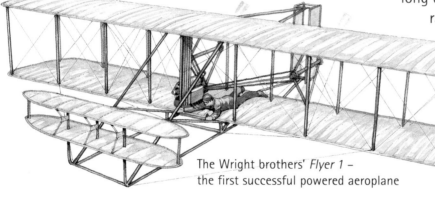

The Wright brothers' *Flyer 1* – the first successful powered aeroplane

Why do aeroplanes need instruments?

A modern aeroplane is a complicated piece of machinery that uses all sorts of different systems such as engines, hydraulics and control surfaces. The pilot needs to know how all these are functioning, and the instruments in the cockpit give the answers. Also, navigational instruments indicate how high the plane is flying, how fast it is going and in what direction.

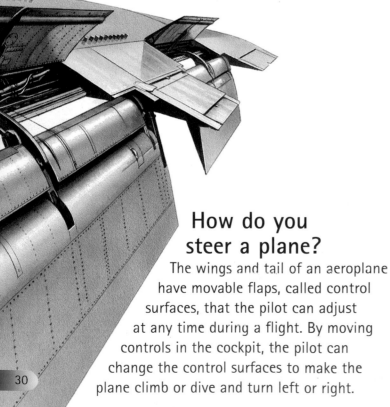

How do you steer a plane?

The wings and tail of an aeroplane have movable flaps, called control surfaces, that the pilot can adjust at any time during a flight. By moving controls in the cockpit, the pilot can change the control surfaces to make the plane climb or dive and turn left or right.

How do planes fly so fast?

The fastest planes normally have jet engines, which create a force in a similar way as when air is let out of a balloon. The engine burns fuel, and forces the exhaust gases out of the back of the engine at high speed. This creates a huge backward force, and the reaction against this force pushes the aircraft forwards.

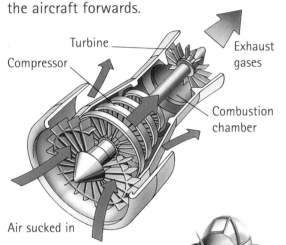

Turbine

Compressor

Exhaust gases

Combustion chamber

Air sucked in

Why does Concorde's nose 'droop'?

Concorde's long pointed nose makes it sleek and helps it to fly faster than any other airliner. But the nose obstructs the pilot's line of vision during take-off and landing so a special mechanism is used to lower it into the 'drooping' position.

Flight position

Take-off and landing position

How can a jet jump?

Vertical Take-Off and Landing (VTOL) aircraft are useful in places where there are no runways. The first aeroplane able to take off vertically was the British Hawker Siddeley Harrier, known as the 'jump jet'. The nozzles of its jet engines, which point backwards in normal flight, swivel towards the ground to give the vertical force needed for take-off.

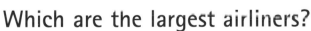

A Harrier 'jump jet'

Which are the largest airliners?

The biggest passenger-carriers are the wide-bodied super jets. The first and best-known is the Boeing 747, often called the 'jumbo jet'. About 70 metres long, it can carry almost 500 passengers and cruises at around 1,000 km/h.

Gliders

Gliders are simple, lightweight aircraft with no engines. They are cheaper to run than powered aeroplanes and have been popular with flying enthusiasts for years. Hang-gliders give an even greater feeling of freedom in the skies. Both types of aircraft are simple, but require special skills and training to fly.

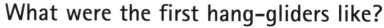

What were the first hang-gliders like?

The first hang-gliders aimed to copy the flight of birds (above), but failed because they focused more on flapping than gliding. German inventor Otto Lilienthal experimented with fixed-wing gliders and made important notes about control surfaces. He crashed to his death in 1896 flying one of his inventions.

How do you control a hang-glider?

The first hang-gliders were steered by the pilot shifting his or her weight towards the desired direction. More modern hang-gliders have tails with movable surfaces, similar to those on full-size aeroplanes, that can be adjusted by using hand controls.

How do you launch gliders?

A glider has no engine so it is pulled along to gain the speed needed for lift. Usually, a powerful car or an ordinary aeroplane tows the glider, and when there is enough lift, the glider pilot releases the tow rope and is able to glide smoothly away.

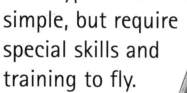

What is an 'aerofoil'?

An 'aerofoil' is the cross-section of a wing that is shaped to produce an upward motion, or 'lift', with little drag. Aerofoils are curved on the top to force air to flow over them quickly, creating lift. The faster the air flows over the wings, the more lift is created, so gliders must fly at a certain speed to stay airborne.

Can you control where gliders land?

Like powered aeroplanes, gliders have control surfaces on their wings and tails, so the pilot can steer an accurate course. In addition they have 'air brakes' that stick out from the wings to provide a steep and speedy descent when it is time to land.

What are microlights?

Microlights are tiny aeroplanes with small engines. They carry one or two people and are made of the lightest possible materials – often aluminium alloy frameworks and plastic body shells. Some microlights have solid fixed wings, but most have flexible fabric wings like hang-gliders. Ultralights are smaller and lighter microlights.

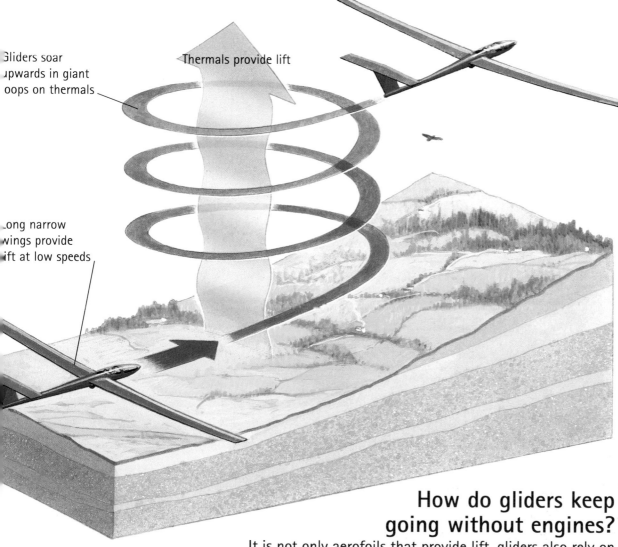

Gliders soar upwards in giant loops on thermals

Thermals provide lift

Long narrow wings provide lift at low speeds

How do gliders keep going without engines?

It is not only aerofoils that provide lift, gliders also rely on 'thermals' (currents of warm air) to keep going without engines. Like birds, pilots search for the thermals, which swirl up into the atmosphere and provide lift. Experienced pilots can stay aloft for hours soaring on thermals.

Quick-fire Quiz

1. Why are gliders towed?
a) Because they have no engines
b) Because they have no pilots to fly them
c) Because their petrol tanks cannot carry enough fuel

2. What are currents of warm air called?
a) Thermos
b) Winds
c) Thermals

3. What are the wings of most microlights made of?
a) Metal
b) Fabric
c) Wood

4. How were the first hang-gliders steered?
a) By the pilot shifting weight
b) By using control surfaces
c) By using steering wheels

Helicopters

Helicopters are the most versatile of all aircraft. They can take off and land vertically and can hover in the air like a bird of prey. Helicopters are built in all sizes, from small craft used for business travel to huge craft used for transportation. Helicopters are also used by the emergency services to get to danger scenes quickly and easily.

What keeps helicopters in the sky?

Instead of wings, helicopters have at least one set of whirring blades, called rotor blades, or 'rotors'. The rotors spin around at high speed, acting like huge propellers to pull helicopters up into the air. This lift effect is reduced by speed so helicopters usually cruise at only 130 to 240 km/h, much slower than most aeroplanes.

Why are helicopters ideal for rescue work?

Helicopters are the most manoeuvrable of all aircraft. In the hands of skilled pilots, helicopters can fly very slowly, change direction easily and even hover directly over one spot, allowing people to be winched on board from below. Helicopters can also land in very confined spaces and so can access awkward rescue sites.

Why do helicopters have extra rotors on their tails?

Without tail rotors, helicopters would spin around in circles. The turning of the tail rotors creates forces that are opposite to the ones created by the main rotor blades, preventing the spinning. The tail rotors are also used for steering – changing the angle, or 'pitch', of the blades alters the direction a helicopter flies in.

What is an 'autogiro'?

An 'autogiro' (right) is an aircraft that has a normal propeller at the front to drive it forwards as well as a set of horizontal rotors. The rotors are not powered like a helicopter's, but spin freely as the aircraft moves to provide lift for take-off. Autogiros, invented by the engineer Juan de la Cierva, were popular in the 1930s.

How are helicopters used in warfare?

In warfare, helicopters are used to transport troops and equipment. This is because they can land and take off quickly in very confined or awkward spaces near battlefields. In fact, helicopters can remain almost motionless when they hover in the air and so sometimes they don't need to land at all. Some military helicopters are large enough to carry vehicles such as armoured cars or troop carriers.

Forward flight –
rotor blades tilted forwards

Backward flight –
rotor blades tilted backwards

Hovering –
rotor blades at same pitch

Who invented the helicopter?

It is thought that many centuries ago, the Chinese made tiny helicopters as toys, but the first serious design for a helicopter as a means of transport was made by Leonardo da Vinci, the artist. His design relied on a screw-shaped wing (right) that aimed to provide lift by winding itself up into the air.

How do you control helicopters?

The pilot of a helicopter controls the aircraft by altering the pitch (angle) of the rotor blades. In the cockpit, there are two controls – the 'collective pitch' and the 'cyclic pitch'. These allow the pilot to adjust the blades to the appropriate position for climbing, descending, hovering or even for flying backwards.

Spacecraft

In 1957, the Russians sent the first satellite, *Sputnik I*, into orbit around Earth – the space age had begun. Since then, astronauts have visited the Moon, and scientists regularly work on board space stations. At first, astronauts travelled in tiny capsules, sent into space by throw-away rockets. Now they use space shuttles – spacecraft that can be used again and again, just like aeroplanes.

What is 'escape velocity'?

The Earth has a strong gravitational pull and so lots of power is needed to get away from the planet and into space. Spacecraft use rockets – the only devices with the power to fly at the speed required to 'escape' Earth's gravity. This speed is known as 'escape velocity' (velocity means speed) and is about 40,000 km/h. Because of the pull of gravity, shuttles do not need the rockets when they return to Earth.

How are space shuttles launched?

Space shuttles are launched by being blasted into the sky by a pair of rockets, which are fuelled from a huge tank that sits between them. When the shuttle has left Earth's atmosphere, the rockets parachute back to Earth, where they are collected and recycled. The fuel tank has to be discarded.

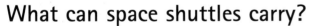

What can space shuttles carry?

Space shuttles are large craft that carry astronauts as well as lots of scientific equipment, which is used to conduct experiments once the shuttle is in orbit. Shuttles also carry satellites, which are released in order to circle Earth. The satellites are used for communications or for sending back information about the weather.

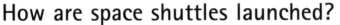

What was first creature in space?

The first creature in space was a dog named Laika (right), who spent a week in orbit on board the Russian *Sputnik 2* in 1957. The first human in space was the Russian astronaut Yuri Gagarin, who left Earth in *Vostok I* on April 12, 1961.

Where do space stations get power?

Space stations run mainly on solar power. They have huge panels of solar cells, called solar 'arrays'. The arrays gather sunlight, which is converted into electricity. This means that space stations do not need to store fossil fuels, such as coal or oil.

Solar panels

Mir space station

Can astronauts travel outside their spacecrafts?

Astronauts may need to go outside their spacecraft in order to perform external repairs. Astronauts wear Extravehicular Mobility Units (EMUs) and must either remain attached to the spacecraft or operate Manned Manoeuvring Units (MMUs). MMUs are special backpacks with rocket thrusters that control direction and movement (left).

What are 'probes'?

Space probes are unmanned spacecraft that collect data. They are able to send back to Earth beautiful images from outer space. 'Fly-by' probes gather information as they pass different planets. 'Orbiters' fly towards a target planet, go into orbit around it and observe it over a long period. Landing probes send down craft on to a planet's surface. Probes use the gravitational pull from planets to travel about.

A Viking probe orbits Mars

Can you drive a car in space?

Yes! Special cars called 'Moon Buggies' or 'Lunar Rovers' (right) have been driven on the surface of the Moon. In 1997, a small rover travelled over the rocky surface of Mars as part of the Mars Pathfinder Project. This rover, the *Sojourner*, unlike the Moon Buggies, was remote-controlled and could journey only a short distance.

Unusual Transport

Some forms of transport cannot be categorized as cars, trains, boats or aeroplanes. New vehicles have come about because of the need to travel in difficult conditions, such as snowy, icy or steep ground. Other machines have developed because people keep on inventing new forms of transport to carry us in ways that are faster, easier or just more fun!

How do you speed through the snow?

In the frozen regions of Canada, getting around quickly can be a problem. Canadian inventor Joseph Armand-Bombardier came up with the answer in the 1930s – a vehicle that had tracks driven by a petrol engine at the back and steerable ski-like runners at the front. These first 'snowmobiles' were used by the army as troop carriers, but today's vehicles are smaller, designed for one person to ride like a motorbike (below).

How do you build a railway where there is not enough room?

Build a monorail! A monorail is a railway that runs on a single rail. There are two main types – ones that run along rails on the ground and ones that hang from overhead rails (above). In some cities, the overhead rail system has been used to save space on the ground.

Which type of transport is the most fun?

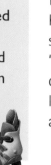

Simple, cheap devices, such as skateboards, rollerblades and ice skates, allow us to speed about and have lots of fun. It is even possible to play sports and perform tricks while using them – but this may take a little practice!

When is drag useful?

Drag is resistance from the air and is a problem for many forms of transport as it slows them down. Parachutists, however, rely on drag for a safe landing. The large 'canopy' of a parachute is the opposite of streamlined – it is large and rounded in order to trap as much air as possible to slow descent.

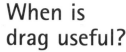

Canopy

Steering lines

What is a 'personal watercraft'?

A 'personal watercraft' is a small vessel like a water-going motorbike, and is known as a 'jetski'. Jetskis carry one or two people quickly through the waves. They are powered by water-jet engines, which force water out of the crafts' sterns, creating forces like the ones from jet engines on aircraft.

How can you travel up steep mountains?

In mountainous areas, a third rail, called a 'rack rail', is laid in between the two normal train tracks. The rack rail is toothed and connects to cog wheels, or 'pinion wheels', under the carriages of the train. This locks the train tight to the track. Cable cars, which travel along cables strung between high towers, are also used as they avoid contact with the ground altogether.

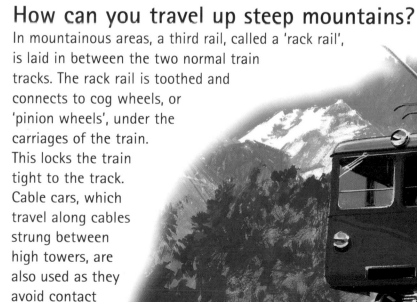

Index

aerofoil 32, 33
air-cushion vehicle (ACV) 27
air-traffic control 30
ambulance 12
articulated truck 11
autogiro 35

ballast tank 24
Benz, Carl 6
Big Boy 14
bullet train 14

cable car 39
camel 4
canal boat 21
car transporter 10
catamaran 21
chopper 19
clipper 22
Cockerell, Christopher 27
Concorde 31
container lorry 10
control surface 30, 32, 33
coracle 21
cowcatcher 15
cruise liner 23

da Vinci, Leonardo 35
Daimler, Gottlieb 18
Décuplette 17
Deepstar IV 25
drag 8, 17, 18, 26, 32, 39

electric power 6, 13, 14, 37
escape velocity 36

extravehicular mobility unit
    (EMU) 37

fire engine 13
Flyer 1 30
Flying Hamburger 15

Gagarin, Yuri 36
Grand Princess 23

hang-glider 32
Harrier 31
Hindenburg 29
hobby horse 16
horse 4, 5
hydraulics 10, 13
hydroplane speedboat 21

ice skates 39

JCB 13
jet engine 7, 31, 39
jetski 39
John Bull 15
juggernaut 10
jumbo jet 31

Lilienthal, Otto 32
limousine 6
litter 5
low-loader 11

maglev train 15
manned manoeuvring unit
    (MMU) 37
microlight 33

military vehicles 13, 24, 25, 27,
    28, 35
Mir 37
monorail 38
Montgolfier brothers 28
Moon Buggy 37
moped 19
mountain bike 17

nuclear submarine 25

outrigger 20

parachute 39
penny farthing 16
periscope 25
pits 9
police vehicles 12

racing bike 16, 17
rack-rail train 39
radar 30
reed boat 20
road train 11
rocket 36
Rocket 15
rollerblades 39
rotor blades 34, 35

scooter 18, 19
scrambling bike 18
sidecar 19
skateboard 39
sledge 4
snowmobile 38

solar power 6, 37
space shuttle 36
space station 37
Sputnik 1 and 2 36
steam power 14, 18, 23
Stephenson, George 15
stirrups 5
submersible 25

tandem 17
tank 13
tanker 22, 23
TGV 14
Thrust SSC 7
tipper truck 10
torpedo 25
tractor 12
travois 4
tread 7, 9, 12, 16, 18
Trieste 25
trike 19
trishaw 17
trolley bus 13
Turtle 24

ultralight 33
unicycle 17

vertical take-off and landing
    (VTOL) aircraft 31
Vostok 1 36

wheel, invention of 4, 5
wheelbarrow 5
Wright brothers 30

Quick-fire Quiz ANSWERS

Page 5 Early Transport
1. b   2. a   3. a   4. c

Page 7 Cars
1. b   2. c   3. a   4. c

Page 9 Racing Cars
1. a   2. b   3. b   4. c

Page 11 Trucks
1. c   2. b   3. a   4. b

Page 13 Special Vehicles
1. b   2. b   3. b   4. c

Page 15 Trains
1. c   2. b   3. a   4. a

Page 17 Bicycles
1. b   2. b   3. c   4. a

Page 19 Motorbikes
1. b   2. a   3. b   4. b

Page 21 Boats
1. b   2. b   3. a   4. c

Page 23 Ships
1. b   2. c   3. a   4. b

Page 25 Submarines
1. a   2. c   3. a   4. b

Page 27 Hovercraft and Hydrofoils
1. c   2. b   3. a   4. a

Page 29 Balloons and Airships
1. b   2. b   3. a   4. c

Page 31 Aeroplanes
1. a   2. c   3. a   4. b

Page 33 Gliders
1. a   2. c   3. b   4. a

Page 35 Helicopters
1. a   2. b   3. a   4. b

Page 37 Spacecraft
1. c   2. c   3. a   4. b

Page 39 Unusual Transport
1. b   2. a   3. c   4. a